Tangled

Learn to draw Rapunzel, Flynn Rider, and other characters from Disney's *Tangled* step by step!

Illustrated by The Disney Storybook Artists
Written by Heather Knowles

Walter Foster Publishing, Inc.
3 Wrigley, Suite A
Irvine, CA 92618
www.walterfoster.com

This library edition published in 2012 by Walter Foster Publishing, Inc.
Distributed by Black Rabbit Books.
P.O. Box 3263 Mankato, Minnesota 56002

Project Editor: Rebecca J. Razo
Art Director: Shelley Baugh
Production Artist: Debbie Aiken

Published by Walter Foster Publishing, Inc.
Walter Foster is a registered trademark.

Printed in Mankato, Minnesota, USA by CG Book Printers, a division of Corporate
Graphics.

First Library Edition

        Library of Congress Cataloging-in-Publication Data

Learn to draw Disney Tangled : learn to draw Rapunzel, Flynn Rider, and other
characters from Disney's Tangled step by step! / illustrated by the Disney Storybook
Artists ; written by Heather Knowles. -- 1st library ed.
     p. cm.
  ISBN 978-1-936309-66-5
 1. Cartoon characters--Juvenile literature. 2. Drawing--Technique--Juvenile literature.
3. Tangled (Motion picture)--Juvenile literature. I. Knowles, Heather. II. Disney
Storybook Artists. III. Title: Learn to draw Rapunzel, Flynn Rider, and other characters
from Disney's Tangled step by step!
  NC1764.L345 2012
  741.5'1--dc22
                                                        2011014026

042011
17320

9 8 7 6 5 4 3 2 1

Table of Contents

Tools and Materials

Before you begin, gather some drawing tools, such as paper, a regular pencil, an eraser, and a pencil sharpener. For color, you can use markers, colored pencils, paint, crayons, or even colored chalk, like Rapunzel!

drawing pencil
and paper

eraser

sharpener

colored
pencils

felt-tip
markers

paintbrush
and paints

How to Use This Book

Follow the steps like the ones shown below, and you will be drawing Rapunzel and the other characters from *Tangled* in no time!

1

First draw basic shapes using light lines that will be easy to erase.

2

Each new step is shown in blue, so you'll know what to add next.

3

Follow the blue lines to draw the details.

4

Darken the lines you want to keep, and erase the rest.

5

Bring your drawings to life with lots and lots of color!

The Story of Tangled

Bells chimed throughout the kingdom; the royal horns blared. And at last, the King and Queen stepped proudly out onto the balcony to present their newborn princess. The crowds cheered happily, and as evening settled in, the King and Queen launched a single floating lantern into the sky in celebration.

But all too soon, the happiness ended. A vain, selfish woman named Mother Gothel stole the infant. For Mother Gothel had discovered a secret: The babe's golden hair possessed the magic to heal—and to keep Mother Gothel young and beautiful forever.

And so the princess, Rapunzel, grew up in a tower hidden in a secret valley. Mother Gothel kept the child from leaving the tower by lying to her. She told Rapunzel that the world outside, filled with ruffians and thugs, wanted to steal her magical gift: her golden hair. The truth was, of course, that Mother Gothel was the thief.

Every year, the kingdom launched a thousand floating lights on the night of the princess's birthday in hopes of guiding her home some day. And every year, Rapunzel watched the lights from the top of the tower, yearning to see them up close.

The day before Rapunzel's 18th birthday, a dashing thief named Flynn Rider was racing through the forest. He'd had quite a day that included stealing the lost princess's crown from the kingdom (something that would bring him a large reward), cutting ties with his cutthroat companions (the Stabbington brothers), and evading the royal guards and all of their horses—except one.

Maximus was the best horse in the royal guard—strong, smart, and relentless. After a wild chase, Flynn escaped the gray and white steed by finding a hidden tunnel that led to a secret valley. In the middle of this beautiful oasis stood a tower.

Flynn climbed up the tower and in through a window at the top. *TWANG!* Rapunzel knocked him unconscious. She and her best friend, a chameleon named Pascal, hid his satchel that harbored the valuable crown.

Seeing this as her only opportunity to get out of the tower, Rapunzel made a deal with Flynn: he would guide her to see the lights and then return her to the tower before Mother Gothel knew she had left; then she would present his satchel to him.

And so, with a reluctant thief to guide her, Rapunzel finally slid down her hair and left the tower. She was thrilled with the outside world. It smelled, looked, and felt wonderful!

Trying to scare her into going back home and reinstating his satchel, Flynn took Rapunzel to a pub called The Snuggly Duckling, which was filled with dangerous-looking thugs! But Rapunzel, realizing that looks can be deceiving, fought against her fear and befriended them all.

Shocked, Flynn found himself bonded to this courageous, spirited, beautiful girl as they, along with Pascal, embarked on the adventure of their lives, which included evading the palace guards, Maximus, the Stabbington brothers, and even Mother Gothel.

One night, after Rapunzel felt she could trust Flynn, she healed his wounded hand with her glowing hair. Flynn was dumbfounded! Rapunzel amazed him.

The next morning, Rapunzel's birthday, Maximus tracked down Flynn. Rapunzel acted as peacemaker between the two. It was her birthday, after all, and she was about to fulfill her dream of seeing the floating lights up close. With Pascal riding atop Max's head, the foursome entered the gates of the kingdom and enjoyed a fun-filled day during which the people of the kingdom celebrated the birth of their lost princess. When evening finally arrived, Rapunzel found her dream in a sky filled with floating lanterns— and in Flynn's eyes. They were falling in love. Nothing could stop them— except Mother Gothel.

With the help of the Stabbington brothers, Mother Gothel set up Flynn and sent him to the palace jail; then she tricked Rapunzel into believing Flynn had left her. Feeling broken-hearted and betrayed, Rapunzel returned to the tower with Mother Gothel.

Luckily, Maximus had witnessed Flynn's arrest. He returned to the pub to get the thugs, who could help Flynn escape. Then Maximus and Flynn galloped off to save Rapunzel.

"Rapunzel!" Flynn yelled from the base of the tower. "Rapunzel, let down your hair!"

The golden hair unfurled and Flynn climbed up, but Mother Gothel was waiting for him. She wounded him gravely. Rapunzel, who was tied up, begged to heal Flynn with the power of her magic hair. But Mother Gothel would not let Rapunzel near him—unless she promised to stay in the tower forever and never try to run away again. Rapunzel gave her word.

But before Rapunzel could heal him, Flynn cut her hair. He would rather die than see this spirited woman live in captivity for the rest of her life. Once cut, the golden locks lost their power. Mother Gothel aged hundreds of years and faded away.

As Flynn closed his eyes, Rapunzel wept. A single golden tear fell upon Flynn's cheek. His eyes fluttered open. The magic was inside of Rapunzel all along. He was healed!

With Maximus and Pascal, Rapunzel and Flynn returned to the kingdom. Overjoyed, the King and Queen embraced their long-lost daughter. It was a love Rapunzel had never felt from Mother Gothel. It was true love. Rapunzel was home at last.

Rapunzel

Rapunzel may have grown up in a tower, but she is full of energy, which she uses to take care of her hair that grew and grew and grew! Her days are full with many things, including reading, cooking, and painting. Her beautiful art covers the walls (and the ceiling!) of the tower. When drawing Rapunzel, don't forget to think of her spirit and her curiosity about the world outside. Even though she could not leave the tower, she dreamed big!

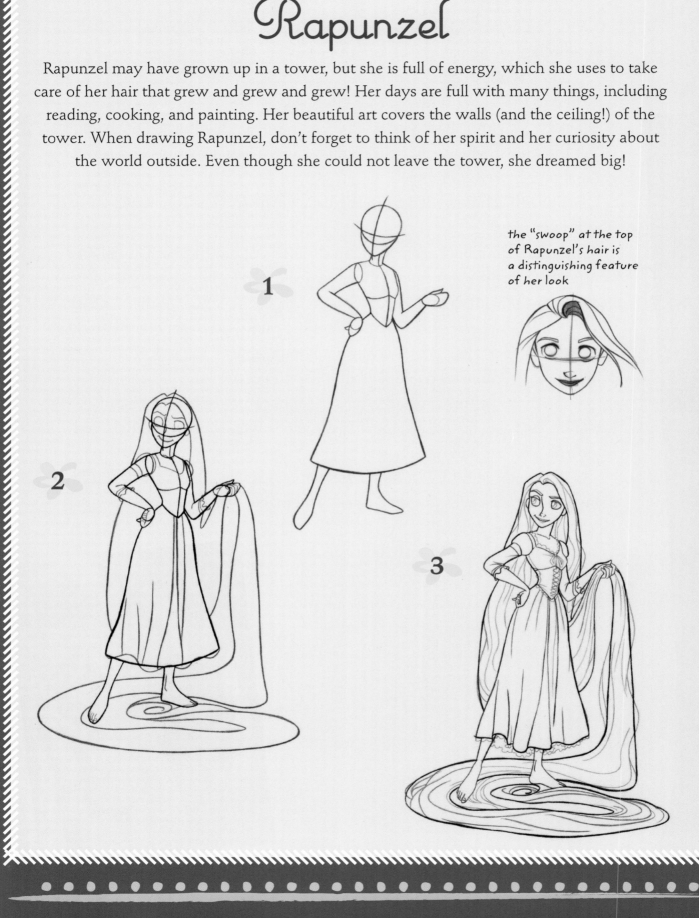

the "swoop" at the top of Rapunzel's hair is a distinguishing feature of her look

1

2

3

Rapunzel's hair has a lot of weight that forms simple shapes

4

NO!

YES!

hair has volume and thickness, even when lying on the floor

Princess Rapunzel

Even after Flynn cuts Rapunzel's hair, she remains the spirited young woman she has always been. Being reunited with her parents is a joy, and she cannot believe how amazing the world outside the tower is!

4

after Rapunzel's hair is cut,
it turns brown and maintains
soft waves along the bottom edges

Flynn Rider

Flynn Rider is a thief. Handsome, charismatic, and slightly vain, he fancies himself rather charming with the women. But he meets his match with Rapunzel. Through the amazing adventure they share together, he decides to change his ways, give up thievery, and become a nice guy.

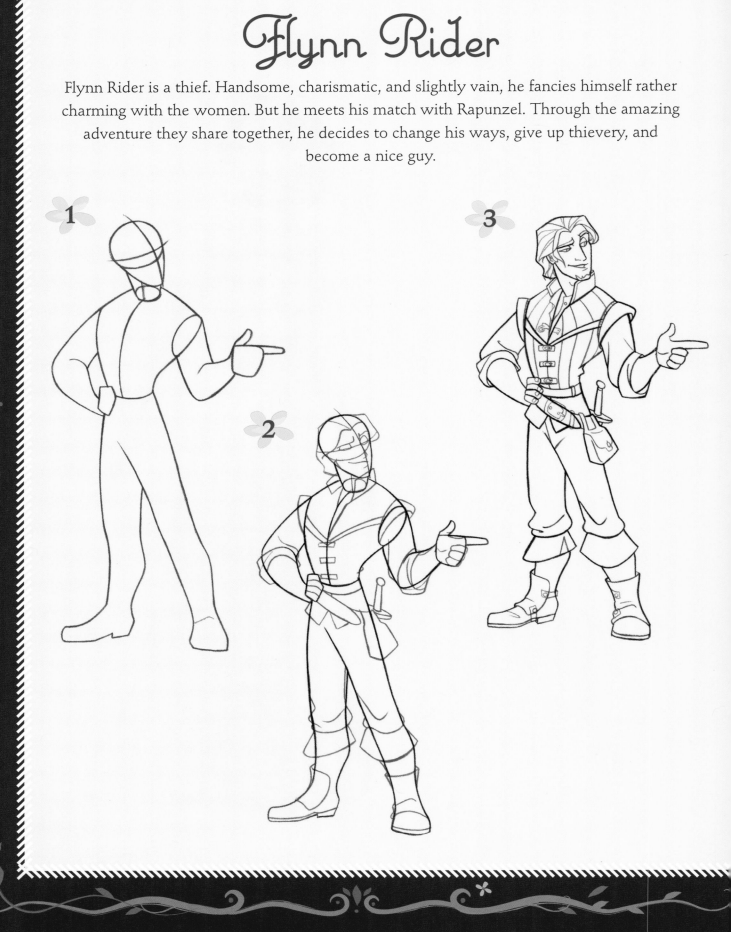

4

Flynn's shoulders are about twice as wide as his hips

Flynn is about 6-1/2 heads tall

Flynn in Action

The thing about Flynn Rider is that Flynn Rider is not really his name!
As a kid, he used to read about a swashbuckling hero named Flynnegan Rider.
Once he meets Rapunzel, he reveals his real name, but he never gives up his superior
athletic skills nor the ability to navigate through tough situations.

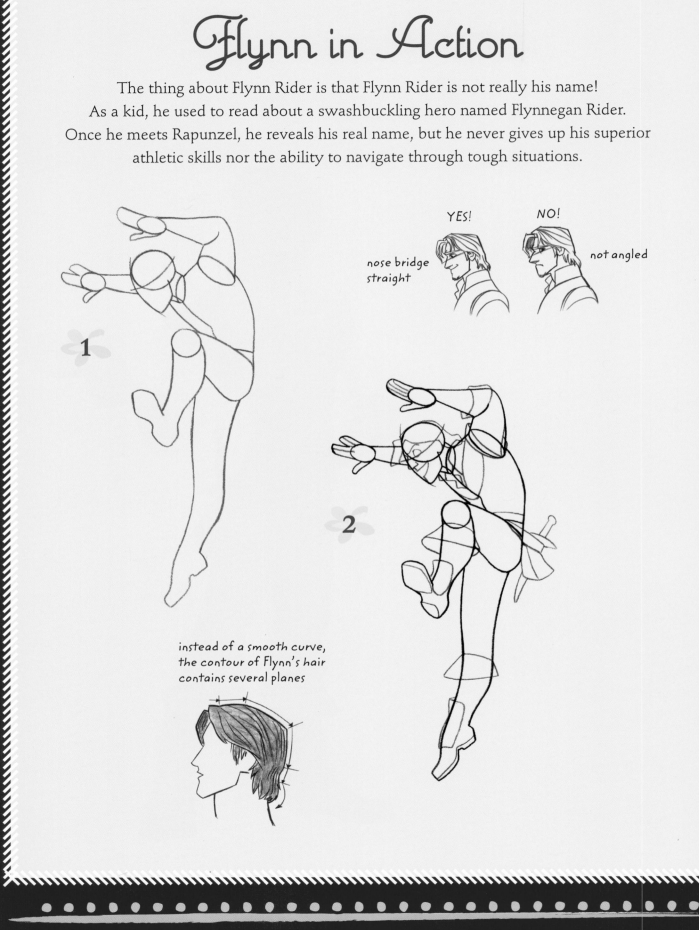

YES!

NO!

nose bridge
straight

not angled

1

2

instead of a smooth curve,
the contour of Flynn's hair
contains several planes

3

4

Pascal

Pascal is Rapunzel's best friend. The friendly chameleon has a way of understanding whatever Rapunzel is feeling—and he reflects it by changing color and expressions. She shares with him her innermost secrets, and she never has to worry that he will tell anyone!

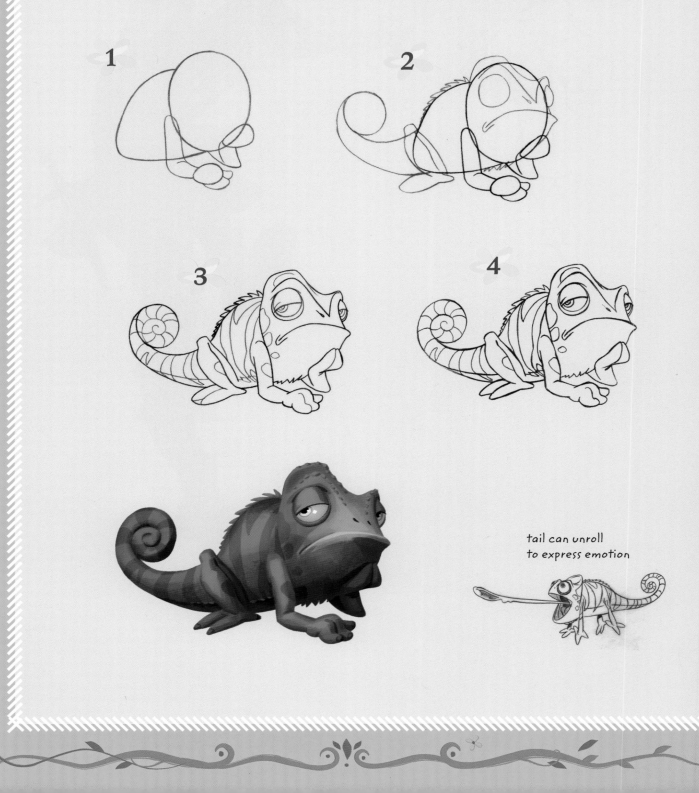

1

2

3

4

tail can unroll
to express emotion

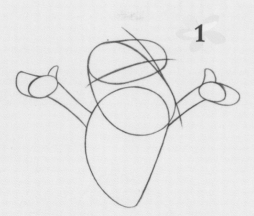

1

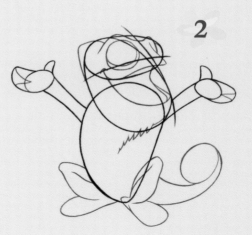

2

3

4

feet have 3 toes

careful with the
shape of the head

NO!   YES!

not like a shark fin   a bit rounded

Mother Gothel

Mother Gothel is young and beautiful—all because of Rapunzel's hair. Some might say that her beauty is not quite as spectacular as she believes. Remember that sometimes beauty is only skin deep, and Mother Gothel's wicked ways show her ugly side in her stance, her expressions, and her cruel comments.

features become more angular and textured when she is transformed into an old woman

4

hair stays contained
in a bullet shape

Mother Gothel is more full-
figured than Rapunzel, with
wider hips and a broader torso

Maximus

As the muscle-bound horse to the captain of the royal guards, Maximus knows he is the finest stallion in the kingdom. Once he gets on Flynn's trail, he uses his strength, stealth, and all five senses to track Flynn down. Though he never speaks, everyone always seems to know exactly what Max is thinking.

1

2

YES! NO!

ears are thin
at the base
and widen

3

when we first meet Maximus, his hair is neat and tied up

4

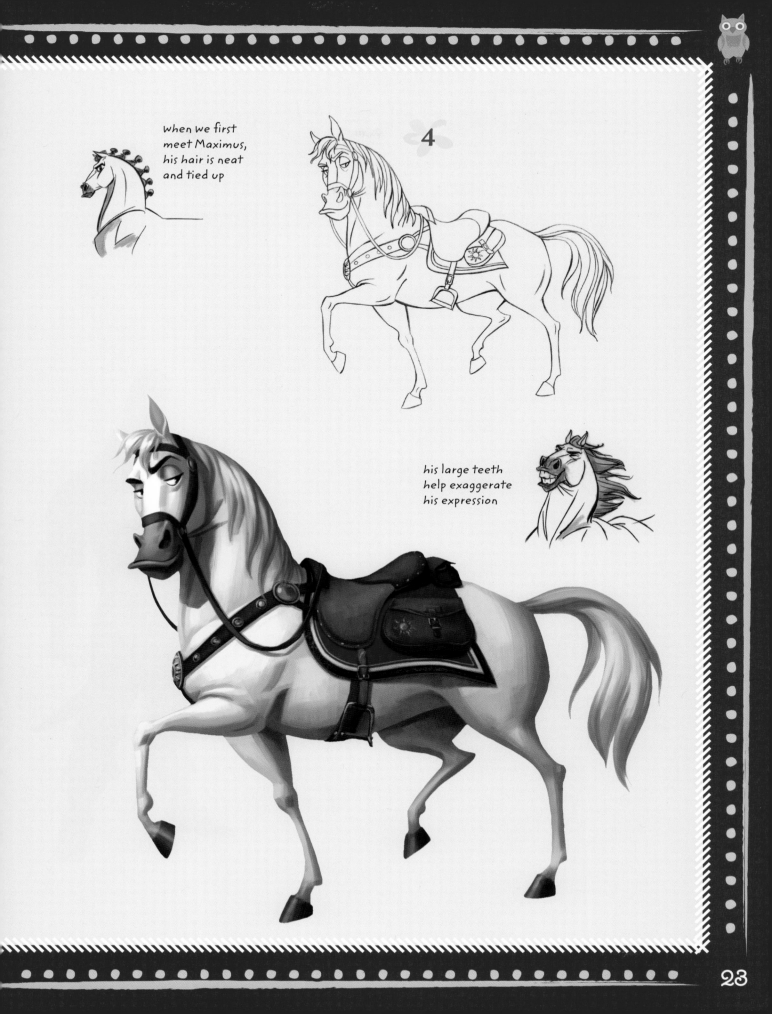

his large teeth help exaggerate his expression

Stabbington Brothers

The Stabbingtons are cutthroats of the worst kind. Almost identical, one difference between them is that the brother without the eye patch does all the talking. But it's clear that they are more comfortable expressing themselves with fists rather than with words.

1

2

hands are thick and blocky

3

4

The Stabbingtons are about 6-1/3 heads high

1

2

3

4

faces are similar, except for scars and eye patch

Atilla Cupcake Thug

With a scary iron mask hiding his face, Atilla is the most intimidating of the thugs. But once you get to know him, you realize that he's actually a quiet softy who is more comfortable in an apron than in body armor. His specialty? Cupcakes, of course!

1

helmet resembles an upside-down bucket

3

2

NO!   YES!

instead of gloves, he wears oven mitts!

4

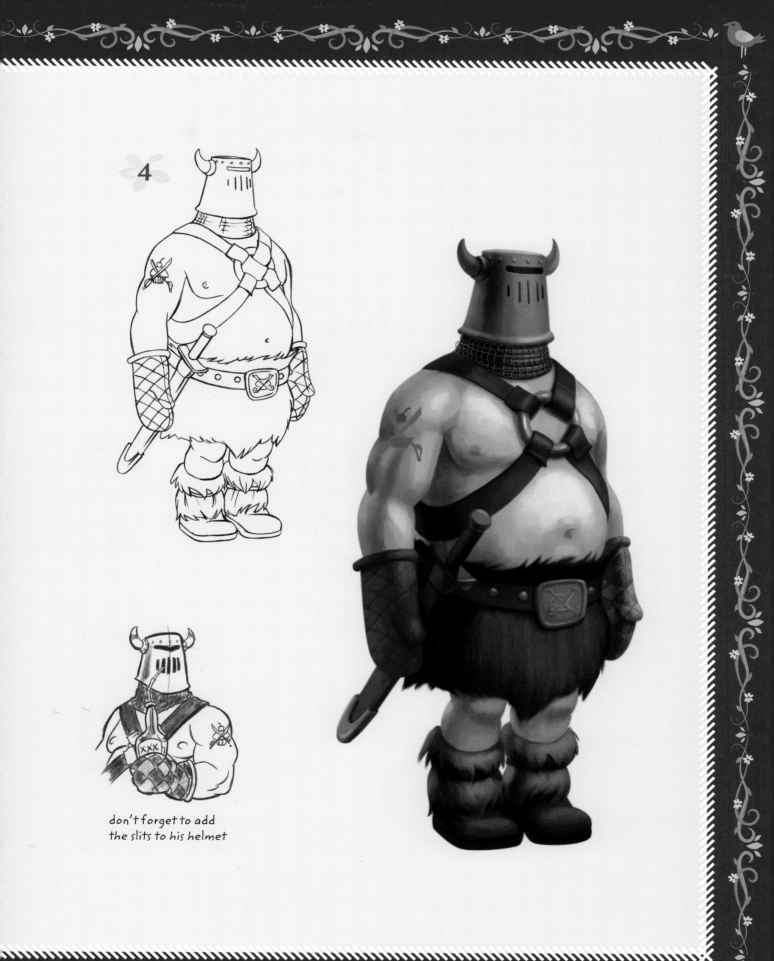

don't forget to add
the slits to his helmet

Killer Sewing Thug

The Killer Sewing thug is strong enough to rip you to pieces, but skilled enough to stitch you right back together again! You'd never know it by looking at this ruffian, but he's really a tailor at heart who is more cut out for sewing, darning, and mending than for fighting, raiding, and looting.

2

1

3

he wears a modified biker's helmet with five spools of thread attached to the top

shoulder pads are
actually pin cushions

4

eyes set high
mouth set low

ponytails extend down
about 1 head's length

Big Nosed Thug

Big Nosed thug isn't the most handsome chap in the pub, but you can't judge a book by its cover. A hopeless romantic, he dreams of finding true love. Maybe one day he'll meet someone who can look past his appearance and see his inner beauty and heart of gold.

1

2

3

NO!   YES!

nose is not sharp like a bird's beak; it's lumpy like an elephant's nose

head shape resembles a football

4

Tor Florist Thug

Tor Florist is a tough thug with a green thumb. At first glance, he appears to be covered in weapons; however, his trappings are really the tools of his craft. He secretly dreams of being a florist and is more likely to plant wisteria in a yard than use his fists in a fight.

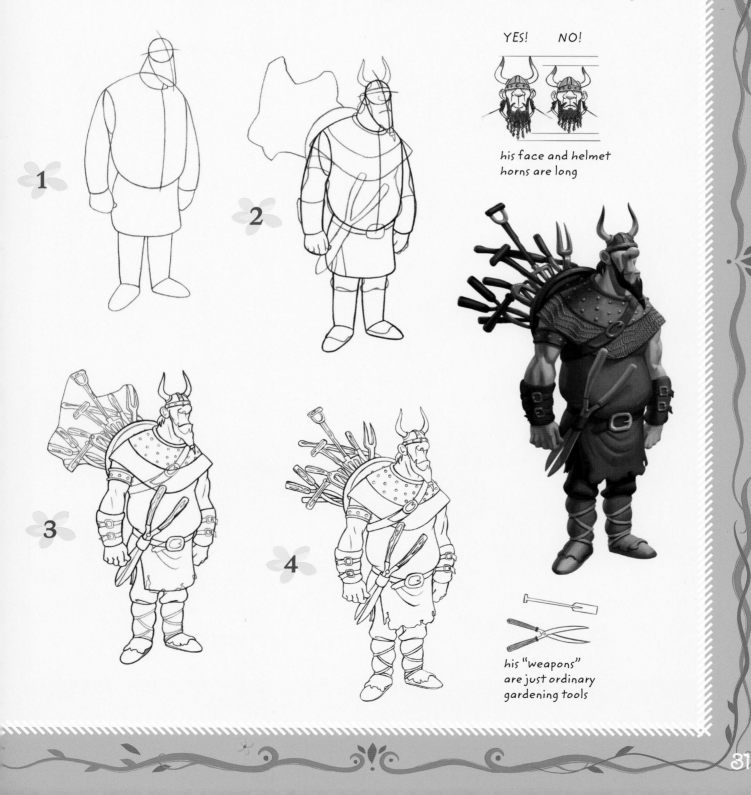

1

2

YES!   NO!

his face and helmet horns are long

3

4

his "weapons" are just ordinary gardening tools

ow it's time to put what you have learned to use! *Tangled* is filled with humor, adventure, and a bit of mystery. Feel free to draw the characters in different settings: the tower, the pub, the forest, the palace—or wherever you want! Rapunzel and Flynn love the large, thick forest trees, which also provide a lot of dark hiding places for evil Mother Gothel and the Stabbington brothers. Maximus will act differently chasing Flynn through the forest than when he is standing at attention with the royal guard in front of the palace balcony. And don't forget the pub thugs. They feel a bit sensitive when they are left out of things, and besides, they are a lot of fun!